Easy Christmas Songbook for Guitar

Book with Audio Access

By
Peter Vogl

For Free Online Audio Access, go to this address on the internet:

http://cvls.com/extras/guitarxmas/

About This Book

This songbook features beginner to intermediate arrangements for classic Christmas songs. These arrangements contain detailed strum patterns and chord progressions that are ideal for playing and singing along. The second portion of this book displays each song along with chord progressions, lyrics, and vocal melody lines. This is a great setup for sing-alongs because the lyrics are written in a large font so that multiple singers and musicians can read along.

Audio Tracks

This course also includes access to audio tracks to help you learn and practice. We have included two different recordings of each song. The first version features the guitar playing along with other instruments. The second recording features the other instruments with no guitar so that you can practice playing the guitar part in context.

You may access these files by going to the following web address:

http://cvls.com/extras/guitarxmas/

The Author

Peter started playing guitar in 2nd grade and very quickly realized his calling. He played in several bands through his years at Okemos High, and proceeded to study classical guitar in college at the University of Georgia under the tutelage of John Sutherland. After receiving his undergraduate degree in Classical Guitar Performance Peter continued with his studies on a assistantship at James Madison University. While there he taught classes as large as 110 people at both James Madison and Mary Baldwin College.

Peter moved back to Georgia and began playing the club circuit in Atlanta as a soloist and with a multitude of bands. He also founded and managed several schools of guitar including the Guitar Learning Center. During this time Peter produced many products for Watch & Learn Inc. such as *The Guitarist's Chord Book, The Guitarist's Scale Book, Intro to Blues Guitar, Intro to Rock Guitar, The Guitarist's Tablature Book, & The Let's Jam! Series.*

In the 90's Peter met Jan Smith and began to play with the Jan Smith Band performing on several of her CDs including Nonstop Thrill, Surrender, and Resurrection. In 2001 Peter moved into Jan Smith Studios where he continues to teach and do session work with local and national talent.

Peter has performed on stage with talents such as Michael Bolton, Cee-Lo, Kelly Price, Steve Vai, Earl Klugh, Sharon Isbon, and Sleepy Brown. In collaboration with the NARAS organization he is the band leader each year at the Heroes Award Dinner in Atlanta.

Companion Christmas Books

These books contain the same songs and arrangements as the *Christmas Songbook for Guitar*. Enjoy the Christmas season with your musical friends as they play and sing along with you.

Each course contains three versions of the Audio Tracks (the instrument by itself, all of the instruments together, and just the other instruments so you can practice playing along in context).

These books are available at your local music store, Amazon.com, on our website (cvls.com), our call us at 800-416-7088.

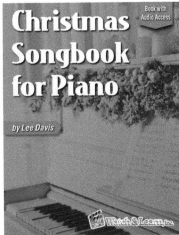
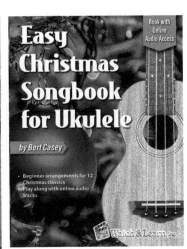

Table of Contents

Section 3 - Lyrics

Section 1
Getting Started

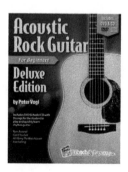

We are including the Getting Started Section from the *Acoustic Rock Guitar* course in case you need to brush up on your technique.

The Guitar

I recommend that you use a steel string guitar for this course. It is important that your instrument is easy to play and is free from buzzes. It's best to keep a fresh set of strings on the guitar as an old set of strings may not tune well and may sound dull to the ear. I also recommend that you start with a light gauge string if pressing down on the strings causes you an inordinate amount of discomfort. You may move up to medium gauge strings as your fingers develop strength and calluses on their tips. If you still experience too much discomfort, you may want to try silk and steel strings, which are lighter and easier to play. Their tone is not the same however, and you will eventually want to move up to steel strings.

Peghead

Tuning Keys

Nut

Neck

Frets

Sound Hole

Pick Guard

Saddle

Bridge

Get to know the folks at your local music store. They can be a great help with supplies, lessons, & advice.

Tuning the Guitar

Before playing the guitar, it must be tuned to standard pitch. If you have a piano at home, it can be used as a tuning source. The following picture shows how to tune the guitar to the piano.

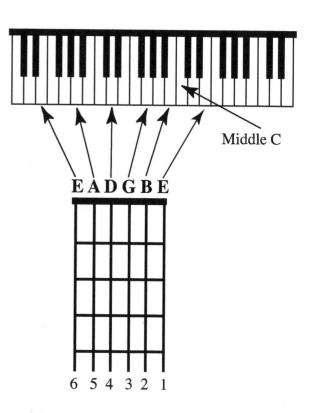

Note: If your piano hasn't been tuned recently, the guitar may not agree perfectly with a pitch pipe or tuning fork. Some older pianos are tuned a half step below standard pitch. In this case, use one of the following methods to tune.

ELECTRONIC TUNER

An electronic tuner is the fastest and most accurate way to tune a guitar. I highly recommend getting one. It may take months or years for a beginner to develop the skills to tune a guitar correctly by ear. The electronic tuner is more precise and used by virtually every professional guitar player.

TIP
Never leave your instrument in a car or trunk during extreme heat or cold.

Guitar Notation

The guitar notation in this book is written on two lines or staves. The top staff is the melody line with lyrics. The bottom line is the strumming pattern for the right hand.

The exercises contain only one line or staff. This is the guitar strumming notation.

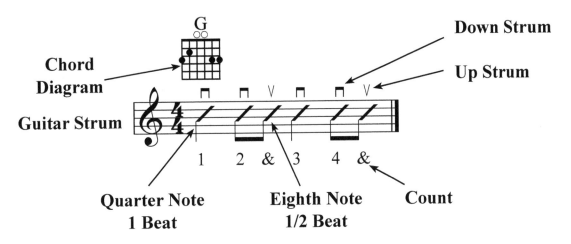

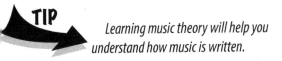

TIP *Learning music theory will help you understand how music is written.*

Holding the Guitar

Casual Position

When sitting there are two basic positions for holding the guitar. The first and most common is the casual position. Sit erect with both feet on the floor and the guitar resting on your right thigh. The guitar should be braced against your chest with the right forearm so that the neck of the guitar doesn't move much when you change hand positions.

Classical Position

The second position is the classical position. Sit erect with your right foot on the floor and your left elevated on a footstool. The guitar rests on your left leg with the neck elevated. This position allows for a better back position and may make it easier for those who have back pain. It also allows for more freedom of movement of the left arm by raising the guitar neck and removing the left leg as an obstacle.

For this course we will be using the casual position, but you should try the classical position and see how it suits you.

Standing Position

If standing and using a strap, keep the guitar elevated for better technique, somewhere around waist to chest high, depending on your build. Use a good strap or it may cause discomfort in the shoulders. A wide strap distributes the weight of the guitar better and is recommended.

TIP *Always use a case or gig bag when transporting your instrument from one place to another.*

The Pick

Selecting the Pick

When you visit a music store, you will notice that there are almost as many pick styles and shapes as there are guitar players. We recommend a medium to heavy pick in a standard shape. Thin picks typically don't produce as much tone or volume. They also break more often.

Holding the Pick

The grip on a pick should provide control while feeling comfortable. The most common way of holding the pick is to curl the right index finger (Figure 1), place the pick in the first joint of the index finger with the point facing straight out (Figure 2), and then place the thumb firmly on the pick with the thumb parallel to the first joint (Figure 3).

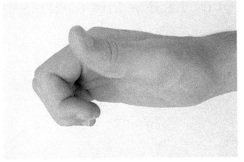

Figure 1

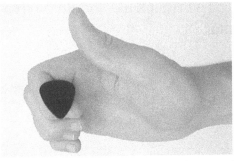

Figure 2

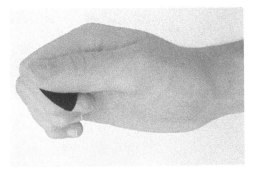

Figure 3

 TIP

Keep many extra picks around. They like to disappear, much like socks.

Right Hand Position

Position the right hand so that the pick strikes the strings between the bridge and the fretboard. The top of the right forearm should be braced against the body of the guitar so that the right hand falls into a position towards the center of the sound hole. Do not rest your wrist or palm on the bridge. Strumming too close to the bridge produces a bright tone and too far forward produces a tone that may be too dark.

Bright   Correct   Too Dark

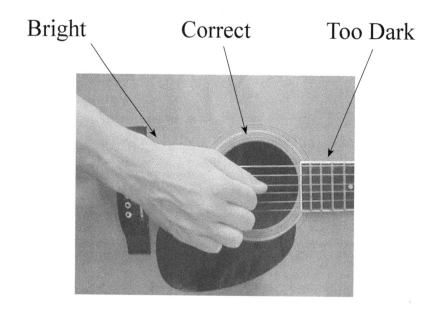

The right hand should be free with no part of the hand or wrist touching the guitar.

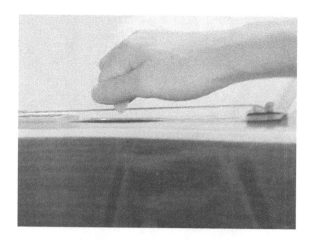

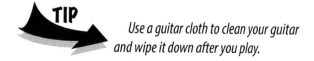 *Use a guitar cloth to clean your guitar and wipe it down after you play.*

Strumming

When you strum the guitar, start with the 6th string and lightly strum down on all six strings, stopping just past the 1st string.

Start Strum   Finish Strum

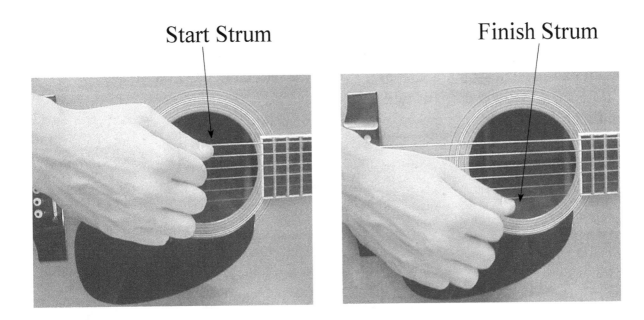

Don't use an exaggerated stroke that carries the right hand beyond the body of the guitar. Finish the strum according to the illustrations above.

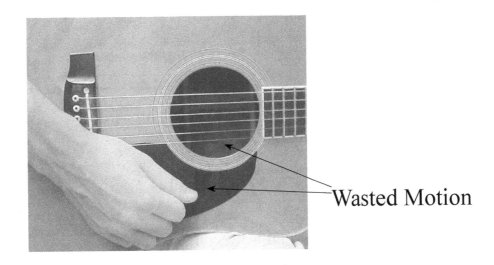

Wasted Motion

Another common mistake is to bang down on the 6th string. Don't make any one string your point of attack. The correct way is to strum down lightly and evenly on all six strings.

 TIP *Don't store your guitar in the attic or basement.*
Extreme dryness or dampness can be bad.

Left Hand Position

When positioning your left hand on the guitar, pay careful attention to several things. The left elbow should hang freely to the outside of the left leg. It is a bad habit to let your left elbow creep into a position resting on the left leg or more into the body. This will avoid undue stress on the elbow and wrist. The hand itself should be positioned so the fingers can stay in front of the guitar neck.

Thumb Position

The thumb placement can vary a little due to hand and body size. Our basic thumb position will be around half way up the back of the guitar neck. This is our *core position*, meaning use this position most of the time. There will be times when we use an elevated thumb position, but this may compromise technique. We will discuss when to do this at a later time. Smaller hands should have an even lower thumb placement. This allows for better stretching and finger dexterity. See the thumb placement exercise on page 12.

Wrist Position

The wrist should be below the guitar neck, which is our *wrist core position*.

A guitar should have a set-up every 6 months or so. Check with you local music store for this service.

Section 2
Christmas Songs

Online Audio Access is available at this address on the internet:

http://cvls.com/extras/guitarxmas

Chord Diagrams

The first song is a three chord song in the key of C and we'll use the C, F, & G chords.

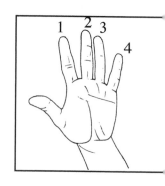

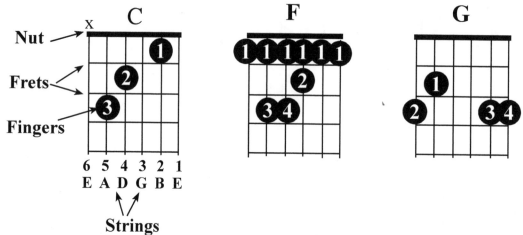

Strum Exercise

The first song is in 3/4 time, which means there are 3 beats per measure and we count 1 2 1 2 3. The strum will be down down up down, down down up down and will be counted 1 2 & 3, 1 2 & 3.

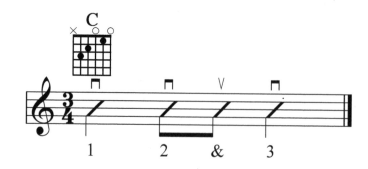

Silent Night

Chords

Auld Lang Syne is a three chord song in the key of G, so we'll use the G, C, & D chords.

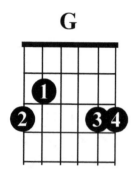 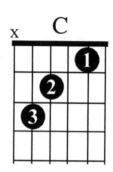 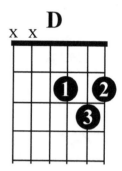

Strum Pattern

This song is in 4/4 time which means there are four beats per measure and we count 1 2 3 4 1 2 3 4. The strum pattern will be down down up down down up and is counted:

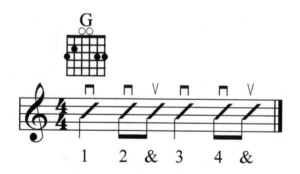

Auld Lang Syne is sung at the stroke of midnight on New Year's Eve.

Auld Lang Syne

Chords

Jingle Bells is a four chord song in the key of F. Using a capo at the 3rd fret will mean playing D, G, A, and E.

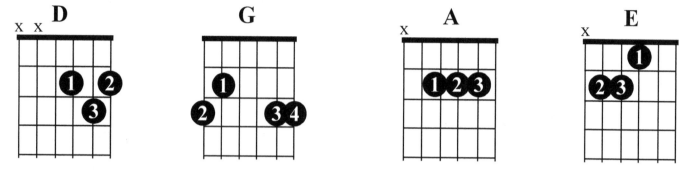

Strum Pattern

This song is in 4/4 time and the strum will be down down down down up and is counted 1 2 3 4 &.

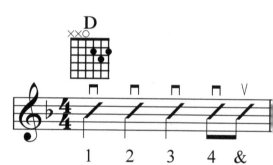

Jingle Bells

Capo 3rd fret

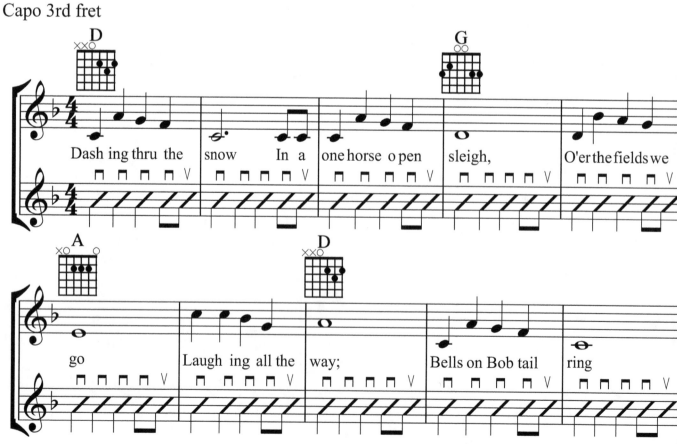

20

Chords

Four new chords in this song: B, Am, Em, and Bm

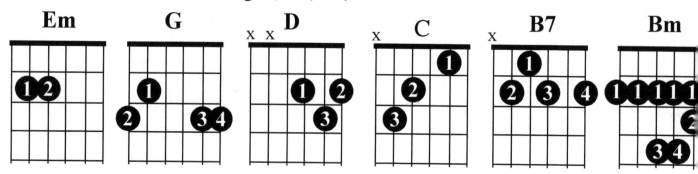

Strum Pattern

3/4 time again. This is the same strum used in *Silent Night* and is counted:

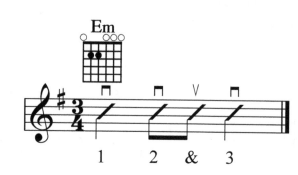

What Child is This

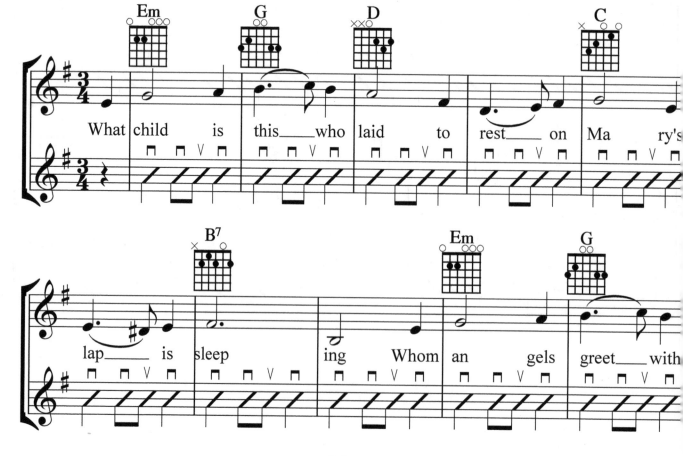

Chords

No new chords for this song, but some faster switching between chords.

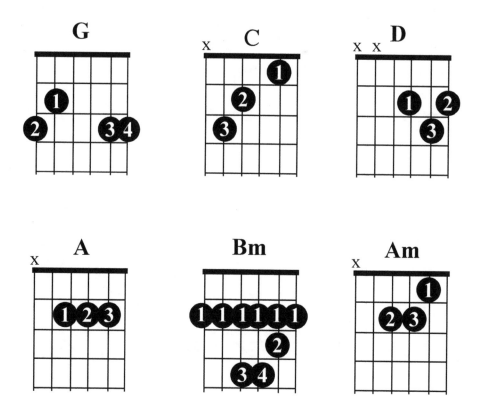

Strum Pattern

3/4 time again and we'll use a two measure strum.

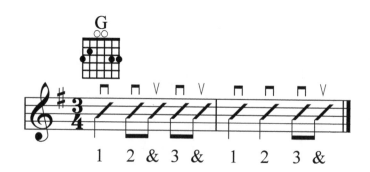

We Wish You a Merry Christmas

Traditional

Chords

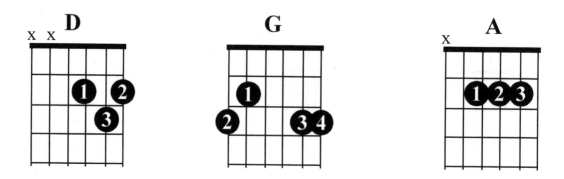

Strum Pattern

No new chords for this song, but we have three different strum patterns to use.

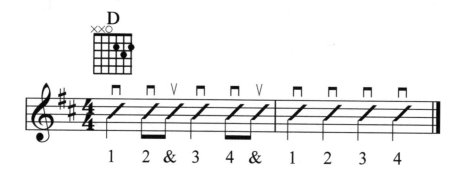

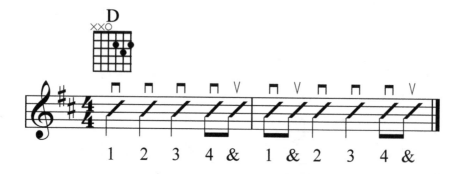

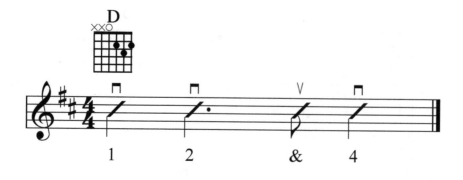

Joy to the World

Chords

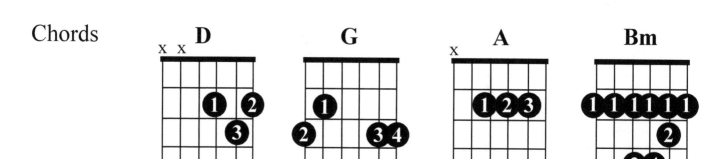

Strum Pattern

There are two strum patterns we will use in this song.

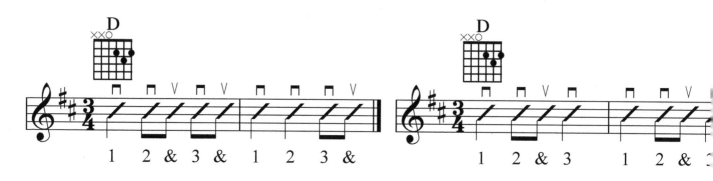

The First Noel

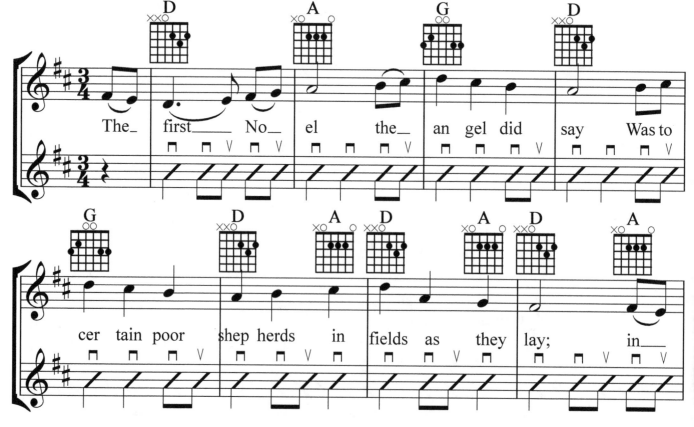

The_ first____ No_ el the_ an gel did say Was to

cer tain poor shep herds in fields as they lay; in____

28

Chords

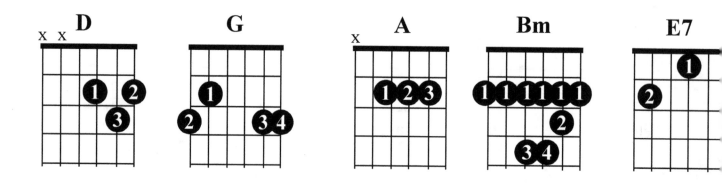

Strum Pattern

We'll use two different strums in this song. The first one we've used before. The second strum follows the rhythm of the melody in the Fa la la la part.

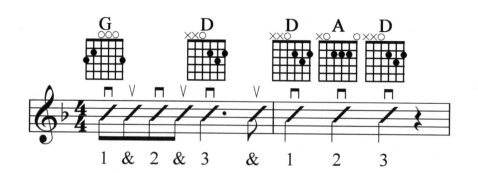

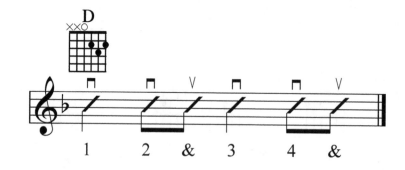

2

Deck the Hall

Chords

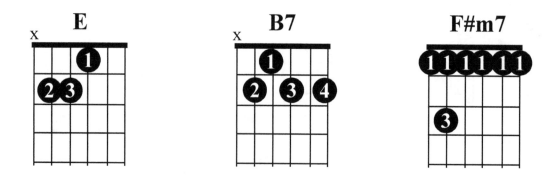

Strum Pattern

Here are the strum patterns we will use for *O Christmas Tree*.

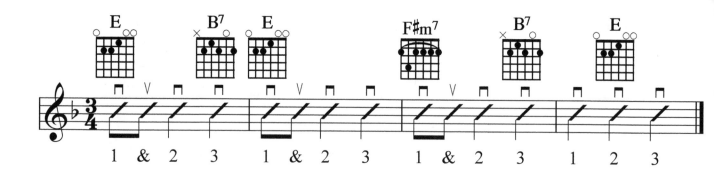

O Christmas Tree

Chords

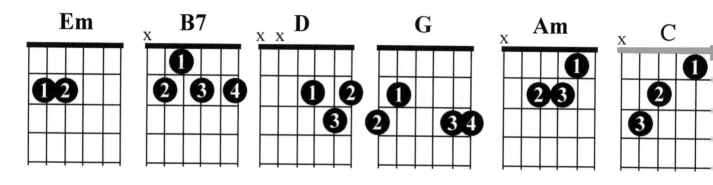

Strum Pattern

Here is the strum pattern for *We Three Kings*.

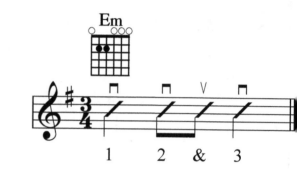

We Three Kings

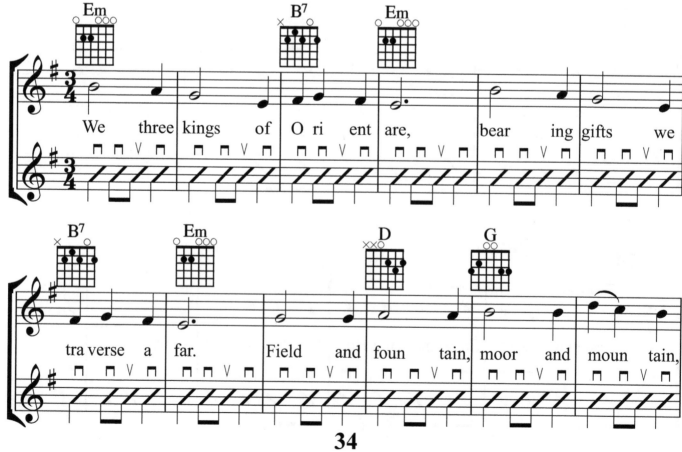

Chords

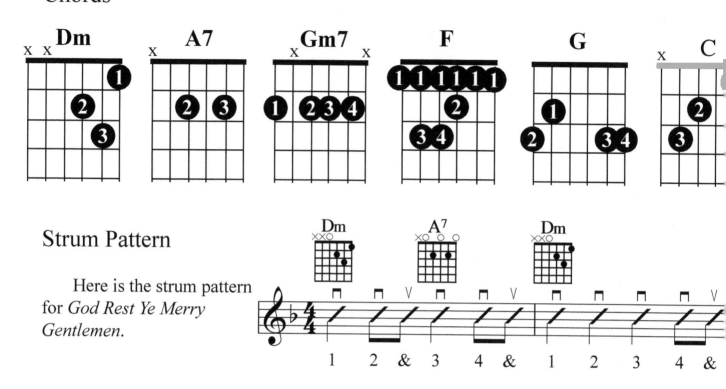

Strum Pattern

Here is the strum pattern for *God Rest Ye Merry Gentlemen*.

God Rest Ye Merry Gentlemen

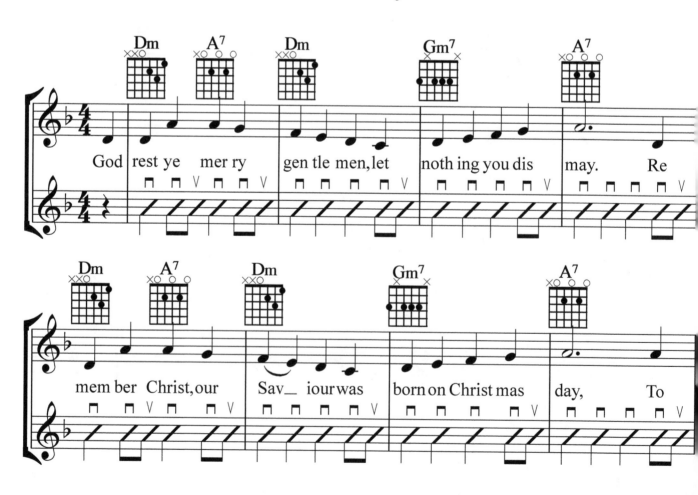

Chords

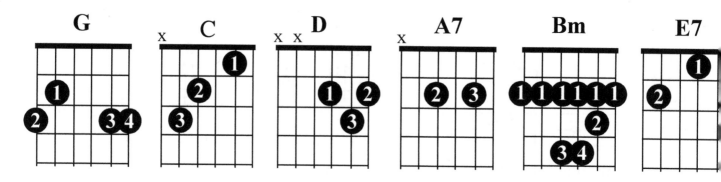

Strum Pattern

Here is the strum pattern for *Hark The Herald* .

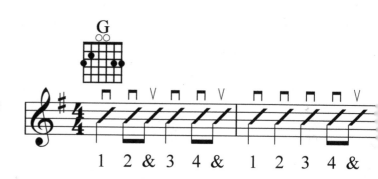

1 2 & 3 4 &   1 2 3 4 &

Hark! The Herald Angels Sing

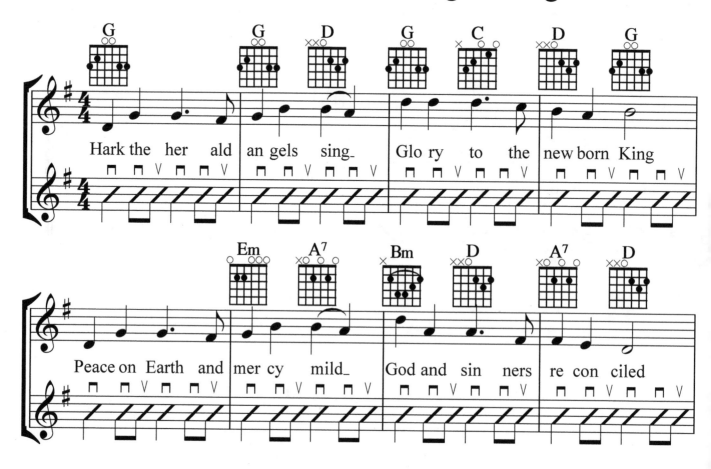

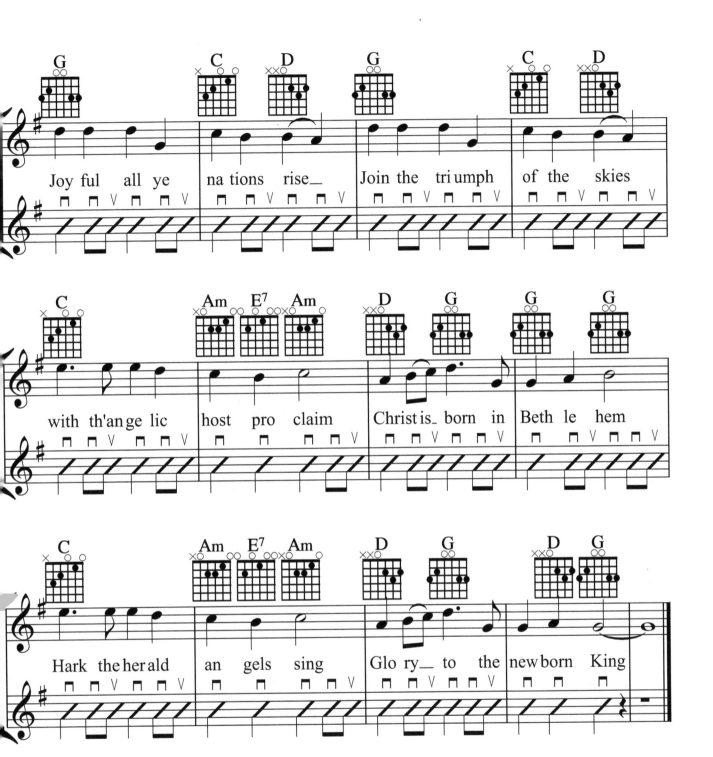

Lyrics

This section contains the melody line, lyrics, and chord progressions so that you can play the complete version of the songs with all of the lyrics. This also works great for jam sessions or playing on stage because the lyrics are in a large font with the chord progression on each verse.

The chords are given as if no capo were used. In this way, the chords will be the same for every instrument. In order to play these songs with a capo, look at the previous section. Playing with a capo may be easier for you and you will still be in the same key as the chords presented in this section.

Auld Lang Syne

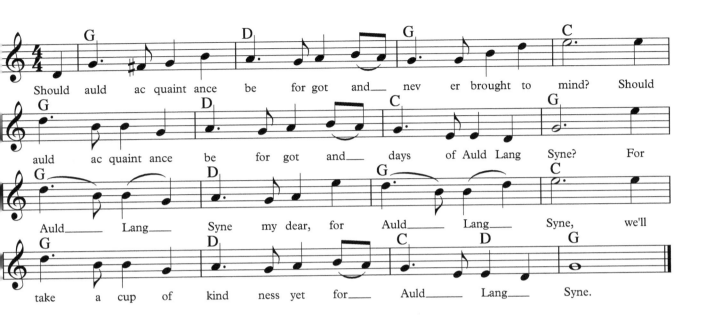

Should ^Gauld acquaintance ^Dbe forgot
And ^Gnever brought to ^Cmind
Should ^Gauld acquaintance ^Dbe forgot
And ^Cdays of ^DAuld Lang S^Gyne
For ^GAuld Lang S^Dyne my dear
For ^GAuld Lang S^Cyne
We'll ^Gtake a cup of k^Dindness yet
For ^CAuld L^Dang S^Gyne

Note - There are other verses to *Auld Lang Syne*, but it's typically performed with only this
erse at the stroke of midnight on New Year's Eve. It's an old Scottish tune and is translated as
old long time". You'll also hear singers substitute old for Auld in the first two lines.

Deck the Hall

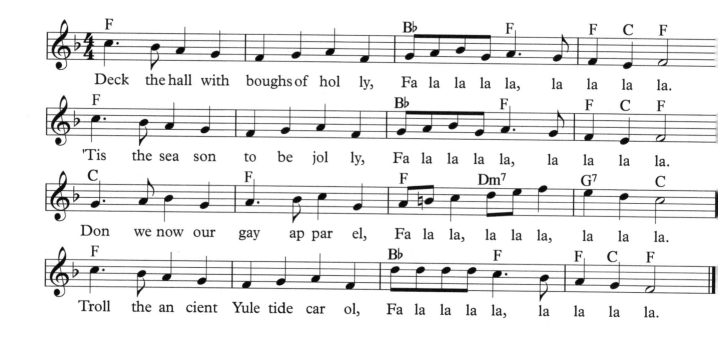

Deck the hall with boughs of hol ly, Fa la la la la, la la la la.

'Tis the sea son to be jol ly, Fa la la la la, la la la la.

Don we now our gay ap par el, Fa la la, la la la, la la la.

Troll the an cient Yule tide car ol, Fa la la la la, la la la la.

Deck the hall with boughs of holly
Fa la la la la, la la la la
'Tis the season to be jolly
Fa la la la la, la la la la
Don we now our gay apparel
Fa la la, la la la, la la la
Troll the ancient yuletide carol
Fa la la la la, la la la la

See the blazing yule before us
Fa la la la la, la la la la
Strike the harp and join the chorus
Fa la la la la, la la la la
Follow me in merry measure
Fa la la, la la la, la la la
While I tell of yule tide treasure
Fa la la la la, la la la la

Fast away the old year passes
Fa la la la la, la la la la
Hail the new year lads and lases
Fa la la la la, la la la la
Sing we joyous all together
Fa la la, la la la, la la la
Heedless of the wind and weather
Fa la la la la, la la la la

God Rest Ye Merry Gentlemen

God rest ye mer ry gen tle men, let no thing you dis may Re mem ber, Christ, our
Sav____ iour was born on Christ mas day To save us all from Sa tan's pow'r when
we were gone a stray O____ tid ings of com____ fort and joy com fort and
joy O____ ti____ dings of com____ fort and joy

God rest ye merry gentlemen, let nothing you dismay
Remember Christ, our Saviour, was born on Christmas day
To save us all from Satan's pow'r when we were gone astray
O tidings of comfort and joy, comfort and joy
O tidings of comfort and joy

In Bethlehem, in Israel, this blessed Babe was born
And laid within a manger upon this blessed morn
That which His Mother Mary did nothing take in scorn
O tidings of comfort and joy, comfort and joy
O tidings of comfort and joy

From God our Heavenly Father a blessed angel came
And unto certain shepherds brought tiding to the same
How that in Bethlehem was born the Son of God by name
O tidings of comfort and joy, comfort and joy
O tidings of comfort and joy

43

Hark! The Herald Angels Sing

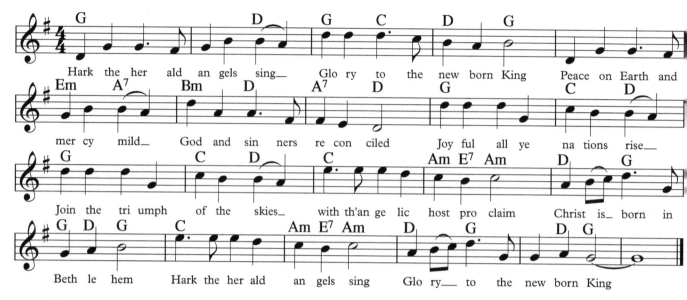

G   D   G   C   D   G
Hark the herald angels sing Glory to the newborn King
G   Em   A⁷   Bm   D   A⁷   D
Peace on Earth and mercy mild God and sinners reconciled
G   C   D   G   C   D
Joyful all ye nations rise, join the triumph of the skies
C   Am   E⁷   Am   D.   G   D G
With th'angelic host proclaim, Christ is born in Bethlehem
C   Am E⁷   Am   D   G   D   G
Hark the herald angels sing, Glory to the newborn King

G   D   G   C   D   G
Christ by highest heav'n adored Christ, the everlasting Lord!
G   Em   A⁷   Bm   D   of the A⁷   D
Late in time behold Him come offspring of the virgin's womb
G.   C   D   G   C   D
Veiled in flesh the Godhead see, hail the'incarnate Deity
C   Am   E⁷   Am   D   G   D G.
Pleased as man with man to dwell, Jesus our Immanuel
C   Am E⁷   Am   D   G   D   G
Hark the herald angels sing, Glory to the newborn King

G   D   G   C   D   G
Hail, the heav'n born Prince of Peace, hail the Son of righteousness
G   Em   A⁷   Bm   D   A⁷   D
Light and life to all He brings, ris'n with healing in His wings
G   C   D   G   C   D
Mild He lays His glory by, born that man no more may die
C   Am   E⁷ Am   D   G.   D   G
Born to raise the sons of earth, born to give them second birth
C   Am E⁷   Am   D   G   D   G
Hark the herald angels sing, Glory to the newborn King

Jingle Bells

D̊ashing through the snow in a one horse open B♭sleigh
O'er the fields we C̊go laughing all the F̊way
B̊ells on bobtail ring making spirits b♭right
What fun it is to C̊ride and sing a sleighing song toFˋnight C̊Oh

J̊ingle bells, jingle bells, jingle B♭all the way
O̊h what fun it is to ride in a G̊one horse open C̊sleigh, hey
J̊ingle bells, jingle bells, jingle B♭all the way
O♭h what fun it is to ride in a C̊one horse open F̊sleigh

A dˋay or two ago I thought I'd take a B♭ride
And soon Miss Fanny C̊Bright was seated at my F̊side
The hˋorse was lean and lank, misfortune seemed his B♭lot
We got into a C̊drifted bank and then we go upFˋsot C̊Oh
Chorus

45

Joy to the World

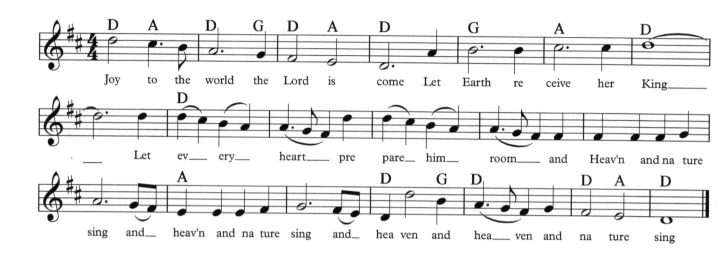

Joy to the world the Lord is come Let Earth re ceive her King____

____ Let ev__ ery__ heart__ pre pare_ him__ room__ and Heav'n and na ture

sing and__ heav'n and na ture sing and_ hea ven and hea__ ven and na ture sing

D A   D   G D A D
Joy to the world! The Lord is come
      G   A   D
Let earth receive her King
      D
Let every heart prepare Him room
And Heav'n and nature sing
      A
And Heav'n and nature sing
      D   G   D   A D
And Heav'n and Heav'n and nature sing

D A   D   G   D   A D
Joy to the world! The Savior reigns
      G   A   D
Let men their songs employ
          D
While fields and floods, rocks, hills, and plains
Repeat the sounding joy
      A
Repeat the sounding joy
      D   G D   A D
Repeat, repeat the sounding joy

D A   D   G   D   A   D
He rules the world with truth and grace
      G   A   D
And makes the nations prove
      D
The glories of His righteousness
And wonders of His love
      A
And wonders of His love
      D   G   D   A D
And wonders and wonders of His love

46

O Christmas Tree

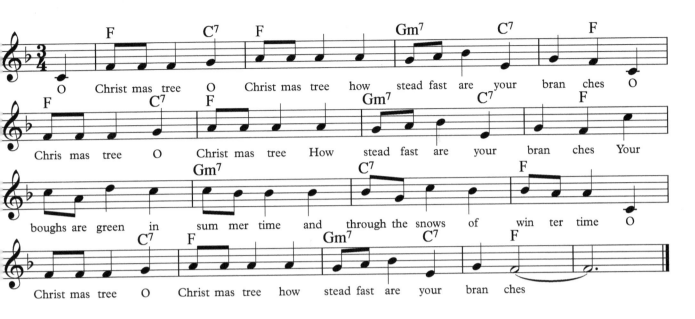

F   C⁷ F   Gm⁷   C⁷   F

O Christmas tree, O Christmas tree, how stead fast are your branches
O Christmas tree, O Christmas tree, how stead fast are your branches
You boughs are green in summer time and through the snows of winter time
O Christmas tree, O Christmas tree, how stead fast are your branches

O Christmas tree, O Christmas tree, much pleasure doth thou bring me
O Christmas tree, O Christmas tree, much pleasure doth thou bring me
For every year the Christmas tree bring to us all both joy and glee
O Christmas tree, O Christmas tree, much pleasure doth thou bring me

O Christmas tree, O Christmas tree, thou candles shine out brightly
O Christmas tree, O Christmas tree, thou candles shine out brightly
Each bough doth hold its tiny light that makes each toy to sparkle bright
O Christmas tree, O Christmas tree, thou candles shine out brightly

Silent Night

Si____ lent night Ho____ ly night All is calm

All is bright Round yon vir____ gin Moth er and Child

Ho ly in fant so ten der and mild Sleep in hea ven ly

peace____ Sleep__ in hea ven ly peace

C
Silent night, Holy night
G   C
All is calm, all is bright
F   C
Round yon virgin Mother and Child
F   C
Holy infant so tender and mild
G   C
Sleep in heavenly peace
C   G   C
Sleep in heavenly peace

C
Silent night, Holy night
G   C
Shepherds quake at the sight
F   C
Glories stream from heaven afar
F   C
Heav'nly hosts sing Alleluia
G   C
Christ the Savior is born!
C   G   C
Christ the Savior is born!

C
Silent night, Holy night
G   C
Son of God, love's pure light
F   C
Radiant beams from Thy holy face
F   C
With the dawn of redeeming grace
G   C
Jesus, Lord, at Thy birth
C   G   C
Jesus, Lord, at Thy birth

48

The First Noel

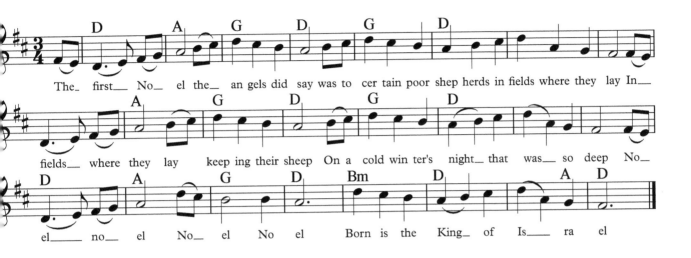

The first ^{D}Noel the ^{A}angels ^{G}did ^{D}say
Was to ^{G}certain poor she^{D}pherds in fields where they lay
In fields where they ^{A}lay keeping ^{G}their ^{D}sheep
On a ^{G}cold winter's ^{D}night that was so deep
^{D}Noel, ^{A}Noel, ^{G}Noel, ^{D}Noel
^{Bm}Born is the King ^{D}of Is^{A}ra^{D}el

They ^{D}looked up ^{A}and saw ^{G}a ^{D}star
^{G}Shining in the ^{D}east, beyond them far
And to the ^{A}earth it ^{G}gave great ^{D}light
And ^{G}so it continued ^{D}both day and night
^{D}Noel, ^{A}Noel, ^{G}Noel, ^{D}Noel
^{Bm}Born is the King ^{D}of Is^{A}ra^{D}el

49

We Three Kings

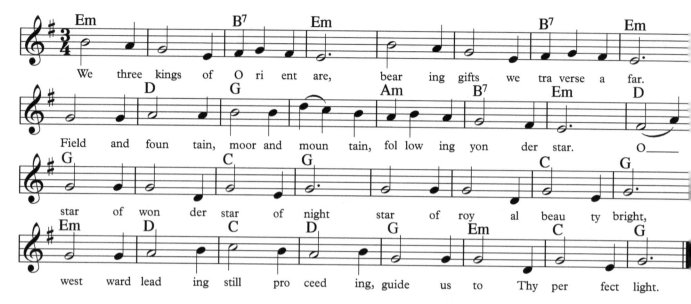

Chorus

Em   B⁷   Em
We three kings of Orient are
                B⁷   Em
Bearing gifts we traverse a far
Em   D   G
Field and fountain, moor and mountain
Am   B⁷   Em
Following yonder star
D   G   C   G.
O, Star of wonder star of night
         C   G.
Star of royal beauty bright
Em   D   C   D
Westward leading still proceeding
G   Em   C   G
Guide us to Thy perfect light

Em   B⁷   Em
Born a king on Bethlehem's plain
           B⁷   Em
Gold I bring to crown him again
Em   D   G
King forever, ceasing never
Am   B⁷   Em.
Over us all to reign

Chorus

Em   B⁷   Em
Frankincense to offer have I
          B⁷   Em
Incense owns a Diety nigh
Em   D   G
Prayer and praising, voices raising
Am   B⁷   Em
Worshipping God on high

Chorus

We Wish You a Merry Christmas

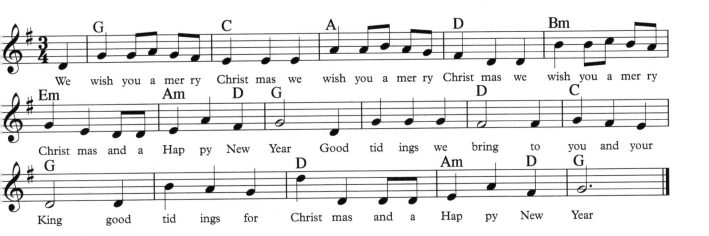

We ^Gwish you a merry C^Christmas
We ^Awish you a merry C^Dhristmas
We ^{Bm}wish you a merry C^{Em}hristmas
And a H^{Am}appy N^Dew Y^Gear
Good ti^Gdings we bri^Dng to y^Cou and your K^Ging
Good tiding for Christmas and a H^Dappy N^{Am}ew Y^De^Gar

We ^Gall want some figgy p^Cudding
We ^Aall want some figgy p^Dudding
We ^{Bm}all want some figgy p^{Em}udding
And a ^{Am}cup of ^Dgood ch^Geer
Chorus

We ^Gwon't go until we g^Cet some
We ^Awon't go until we g^Det some
We ^{Bm}won't go until we g^{Em}et some
So b^{Am}ring some ^Dright h^Gere
Chorus

What Child is This

What child is this who laid to rest on Ma ry's lap is sleep ing Whom

an gels greet with an thems sweet while shep herds watch are keep ing

This, this is Christ the King whom shep herds watch and an gels sing

Haste haste to bring him laud The Babe the son of Ma ry

What ^{Em} child is ^G this who la^Did to rest
On ^C Mary's lap is sle^Beping
Whom ^{Em} angels ^G greet with a^Dnthems sweet
While ^C shepherds ^B watch are ke^{Em}eping
^{Bm} This, ^G this is ^D Christ the King
Whom ^{Em} shepherds ^{Am} watch and ^B angels sing
^{Bm} Haste, ^G haste to ^D bring him laud
The ^{Em} Babe, the ^B son of ^{Em} Mary

So ^{Em} bring him incense, ^G gold, and ^D myrrh
Come, ^C peasant, king to ^B own Him
The ^{Em} King of Ki^Gngs salv^Dation brings
Let ^C loving hearts ^B enthrone ^{Em} Him
^{Em} Raise, ^G raise the ^D song on high
The ^C virgin sings her ^B lullaby
^{Em} Joy, ^G joy, for ^D Christ, is born
The ^C Babe the ^B son of ^{Em} Mary

Chord Chart

There is a chord chart on the following page that shows all of the common chords you will encounter. Notice that they are laid out in sequence with all of the different type chords on the same line. For instance, all of the different G chords are on the first line. They are also aligned vertically in finger patterns. For example, all of the 7th chords are in the third column.

The small x on top of the chord diagram means don't strum this string because it would be a note that is not in the chord.

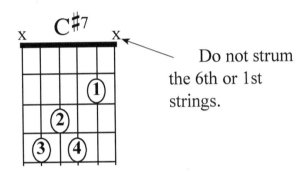

Do not strum the 6th or 1st strings.

The Roman numeral at the right side of the chord shows the fret position of the index finger.

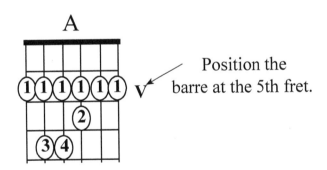

Position the barre at the 5th fret.

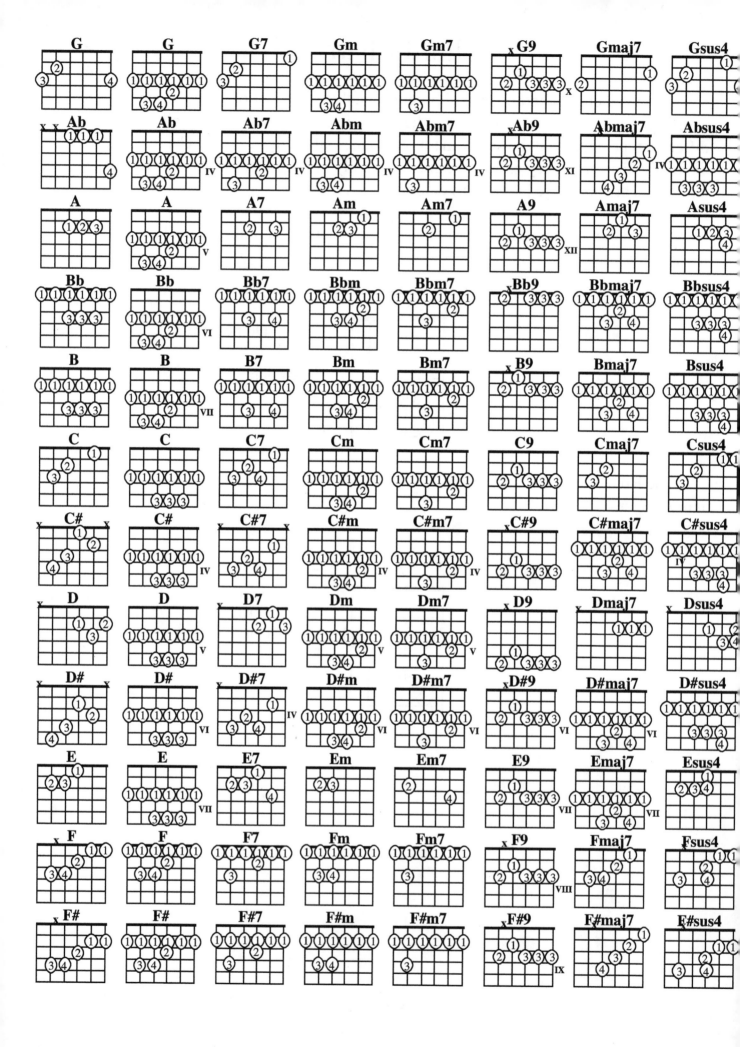

Other Books by Peter Vogl

The *Guitarist's Chord Book* by Peter Vogl contains over 900 chords with photos to clearly illustrate each chord and each note of the chord is labeled. This book makes finding chords you want to play easy. It also contains a special moveable chords section with the most widely used shapes for each class of chord. Peter has also included goodies from his bag of tricks to give you new sounds, shapes, and inspirations for song arrangements. This is a must read for guitar players of all levels.

The *Guitarist's Scale Book* by Peter Vogl is a complete scale encyclopedia for guitar with over 400 scales and modes. It contains scale diagrams with notation and tablature for each scale and tips on how and when to use each scale. This scale book also contains outside jazz scales, exotic scales, Peter's own Cross-Stringing scales, and easy to understand explanations of scales and modes. This is the only guitar scale book you'll ever need.

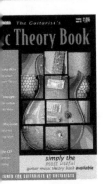

The *Guitarist's Music Theory Book* by Peter Vogl is the first music theory book designed for guitar by a guitarist. The book explains music theory as it applies to the guitar and covers intervals, scales, chords, chord progressions, and the Nashville Number System. You will also get online access to audio examples of all the music in the book and also an ear training section. This book was written to help all guitar players achieve a better understanding of the guitar and of the music they play.

The *Creating Acoustic Guitar Solos Book with Video & Audio Access* by Peter Vogl will teach you how to play a series of acoustic guitar solos. You will combine chords and fast single note lines, use a variety of scales and arpeggios, pick finishing notes that match the music, and cover techniques like slides, hammer-ons, double stops, and more. As you move through the lessons, you will pick up the difficulty and speed while also moving around the neck. The solos taught in this course can work as individual pieces or be tied together as an epic solo. The online access includes over two hours of video lessons along with audio jam tracks.

These books are available at your local music store, Amazon.com, on our website (cvls.com), our call us at 800-416-7088.

CPSIA information can be obtained
at www.ICGtesting.com
Printed in the USA
FFHW012110161019
55591732-61409FF

9 781940 301150